Clothes *for a* CORONATION

Illustrated by *Vanessa* CLEALL   Written by *Fiona* MACDONALD

PICCOLO

PAN MACMILLAN CHILDREN'S BOOKS

CONTENTS

© The Salariya Book Company MCMXCIII

First published in 1993 by
PAN MACMILLAN CHILDREN'S BOOKS
A division of Pan Macmillan Limited
Cavaye Place London SW10 9PG

ISBN 0-330-326872

A CIP catalogue record for this book is available
from the British Library.

Printed in Hong Kong

Designed and produced by   DAVID SALARIYA
Editor   VICTORIA POWER
Consultant   ROSEMARY HARDEN

INTRODUCTION

*T*HE CORONATION OF QUEEN ELIZABETH II in 1953 was a spectacular event – one of the tradition-filled pageants that British royalty and aristocracy perform so well. On a cold June day in London, over 7,000 of the most powerful men and women in the Commonwealth assembled to witness their new Queen being crowned. It was a thrilling and moving historic occasion. The Queen was young, solemn and sincere. It was an opportunity for the whole nation to celebrate being British at a time when the recent hard-won victory in the Second World War seemed to have resulted only in economic depression and drabness.

This book describes the events leading up to the coronation, and explains the procedures of the centuries-old coronation service itself. It concentrates, however, on the extravagant and beautiful clothes and robes worn by the Queen and other leading figures in the coronation ceremony and on the priceless British Crown Jewels. Who designed them? What were they made of? Why were they worn? What was their impact on people hungry for glamour and luxury? And what did they tell the world about Britain and the Queen?

HOW TO ASSEMBLE THE DOLLS

The Queen Elizabeth II and Prince Philip dolls come with their own stands, which should be cut out as part of the dolls. Fold back the large tabs on either side of the bottom of the dolls. Use scissors to make small cuts on the tabs, as directed. Slot the left-hand tab into the top of the right-hand tab and the doll should stand on its own.

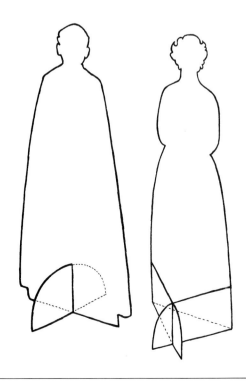

The other dolls need the half-circle shaped stands seen on pages 11, 15, 17 and 23. Cut them out and make small cuts in the top where directed. Then make a small cut between the feet of each doll where directed (but not on the Queen or Prince Philip dolls) and slot the doll into the top of the stand as illustrated.

THE KING IS DEAD

IT WAS 7.30 a.m. on the morning of 6 February 1952. King George's valet walked briskly across the carpeted floor of a downstairs bedroom in Sandringham House. The royal family was staying here, on their private estate in Norfolk, for a short holiday. They came to Norfolk most winters, to enjoy peace and quiet and to go pheasant shooting. As usual, the valet went over to the windows and drew the curtains, to let the dawn light rouse the sleeping King. But this morning, the King would not wake up. Doctors hurried to his bedside, but there was nothing they could do. King George VI of England, who had been ill for months with incurable lung cancer, had died peacefully during the night. He was only fifty six.

The nation was shocked. King George and his Queen, now Queen Elizabeth the Queen Mother, were popular figures. They had won people's respect by their courage and cheerfulness during the Second World War. And, although the King's illness had been diagnosed in 1951, few people – not even the King himself – had been told that he was dying. What would happen to Britain and the Commonwealth now he had gone?

King George's heir was his daughter, Elizabeth Alexandra Mary. She was still a young woman, just twenty five, when he died. On that dismal day in February, she was not even in the country. Princess Elizabeth and the Duke of Edinburgh had set off on 31 January for a Commonwealth tour. They were staying at the Treetops Hotel in Kenya on the night when the Princess became Queen. Hastily, she was summoned back to Britain. On board the plane, she changed into dark mourning clothes. The Prime Minister, Winston Churchill, met the young Queen Elizabeth at London Airport. He wept bitterly, but she managed successfully to conceal her grief. Her first words uttered as Queen on English soil were simple and dignified. "This is a very tragic homecoming," she said.

"QUEEN OF TOMORROW"

ELIZABETH WAS BORN on 21 April 1926. From the age of eleven, she spent most of her time preparing for the day she would be Queen. Private tutors gave her lessons in English, maths, history, geography, French, German, politics and law. Encouraged by her parents and religious advisers, she developed a strong sense of public duty, and took a keen interest in current affairs. To relax, the Princess played the piano, sang, and watched films in Buckingham Palace's own cinema. She liked dancing, boating, horse riding and rifle shooting. For several years, she produced and starred in Christmas pantomimes to amuse her friends at Windsor Castle.

There were more purposeful pleasures, as well. She became a Girl Guide and a Ranger. During the war, she volunteered to join the army, where she enjoyed learning how to drive and repair heavy lorries. Although her parents tried to shield Princess Elizabeth from too much publicity, her broadcasts and public appearances aroused tremendous interest all around the world. In the 1940s, as "Queen of Tomorrow", she represented Britain's hopes for the future. There was a scandal when "Crawfie", a retired royal governess, published her memoirs. Many people said they disapproved, but read the book eagerly all the same.

Public interest mounted to fever pitch when, on 20 November 1947, Princess Elizabeth married Prince Philip of Greece. Prince Philip, who was given the title Duke of Edinburgh the day before the wedding, was a member of the exiled Greek royal family. He had spent most of his life in Britain and was a serving officer in the Royal Navy. For many, the royal wedding provided a glamorous escape from everyday life. The bride was young, just twenty one, and, as the newspapers said, "full of charm". The groom was described as handsome and brave. It took 350 women seven weeks to make the wedding dress, hand-sewn with seed pearls and crystals. Top American stores bribed and begged for advance details of the dress, but the secret stayed safe. After the wedding, the dress was exhibited in London and major British cities. In London alone, 261,832 people queued to see it. The money collected was given to charity.

BOOSTING BRITAIN

KING GEORGE VI died on 6 February 1952, but his daughter's coronation did not take place until 2 June 1953. Why was there such a long delay? For two main reasons – the need to mourn the King and the need to make preparations for the ceremony itself.

The coronation ceremony was not necessary to make Princess Elizabeth the lawful British Queen. She had been that ever since the unknown moment in the middle of the night when her father died. But even if it was not required by law, the coronation was still very important. As a religious ceremony, it blessed the new Queen and gave her the opportunity of promising before God to rule her people wisely and well. Coronations before the reign of George IV (1820–1837) had been quiet, private occasions. But since then, governments had recognised that they were politically useful as well. They brought together powerful people from Great Britain and the Empire (later, the Commonwealth). They would acknowledge the new King or Queen and confirm Britain's status as a leading world power.

There was one more reason for turning the coronation into a public event. It would be good for business. The glittering ceremony boosted the image of Britain at home and abroad. As Prince Philip – who took a leading part in planning it – proudly exclaimed, "We will show you something...which can be seen nowhere else in the world."

Plans and Practising

T HE CORONATION WAS ARRANGED with military precision. Many members of the organising team had had recent experience of war, and they used this to help them plan ahead. They drew up a detailed map of Westminster Abbey, where the coronation was to take place, complete with different coloured pins. Each pin represented one of the participants. Their movements were discussed and plotted in advance, rather like battleship manoeuvres. This was the first coronation to be televised; the organisers knew that any mistakes would be seen by millions of viewers.

The Duke of Norfolk, as Earl Marshal, was in charge. (The earliest member of his family to hold the title of Earl Marshal was John Howard, Duke of Norfolk, who in 1483 was instructed by Richard III to prepare Westminster Abbey for his coronation.) As well as overseeing the ceremony, the Earl Marshal had to arrange seating (2,000 chairs and 5,700 stools) and accommodation for many distinguished visitors who had been invited to attend. Seven ocean-going liners were moored in the River Thames as floating hotels. The Duke also had to consider security and crowd control. A total of 29,200 troops and 15,000 police took part; some marched or played music – there were twenty bands – while others lined the streets. They came from all over the Commonwealth and were lodged in tents in London parks. At the Abbey, the Duke arranged for five medical stations, fifty-two telephones and an emergency tailoring service to be installed. Plans were made to press uniform trousers, so every serviceman would look his best.

The Queen practised her part in the ballroom at Buckingham Palace. She listened to recordings of her father's coronation, so that she could get the timing right and learn her words. Along with her Ladies in Waiting, she walked around with sheets pinned to her shoulders, to become used to the feeling of a robe with a train. She wore the heavy St Edward's Crown – which weighs over two kilos – for tea with her children and sometimes even while feeding her dogs.

THE GREAT DAY

CORONATION DAY, 2 JUNE 1953, dawned cold and grey. It was, as one onlooker said, "the meanest June day" anyone had ever seen. But the weather did not discourage the vast crowds that lined the twenty kilometre royal route. Over 130,000 people camped out on the streets overnight, to be sure of a good view.

There was plenty to see. The service did not start until late morning, but the first guests reached Westminster Abbey soon after 6 a.m. Leading politicians from seventy countries had been invited, along with British peers and peeresses. They travelled in four thousand chauffeur-driven cars, and, to avoid traffic jams, were told exactly when to arrive and depart. Food was provided, but many guests took their own picnics, hidden in their coronets or the folds of their robes.

Distinguished Commonwealth guests travelled as part of the royal procession. Following tradition, members of the royal family arrived after everyone else. The Queen, accompanied by Prince Philip, arrived last of all. They left Buckingham Palace at 10.26 a.m., travelling in the splendid, although not very comfortable, State Coach used for every coronation since 1820. It is made of carved oak covered in gold leaf, with crimson velvet seats. Eight horses are needed to pull it since it weighs about four tonnes.

At 11.15 a.m., the Queen entered the Abbey, to the sound of the 400-strong choir singing Psalm 122. The solemn service began. All through the emotional, exhausting six-hour ritual the Queen impressed spectators by her calm.

On the homeward journey, rain caused problems; coaches skidded and dye streamed from the breeches worn by royal footmen, marking their clean white stockings with splashes of red. But no one cared. The feeling of excitement was too strong. At 5.05 p.m. the gold coach returned to Buckingham Palace. Soon afterwards, the entire royal family appeared on the balcony, smiling and waving to the cheering crowds below.

EⅡR

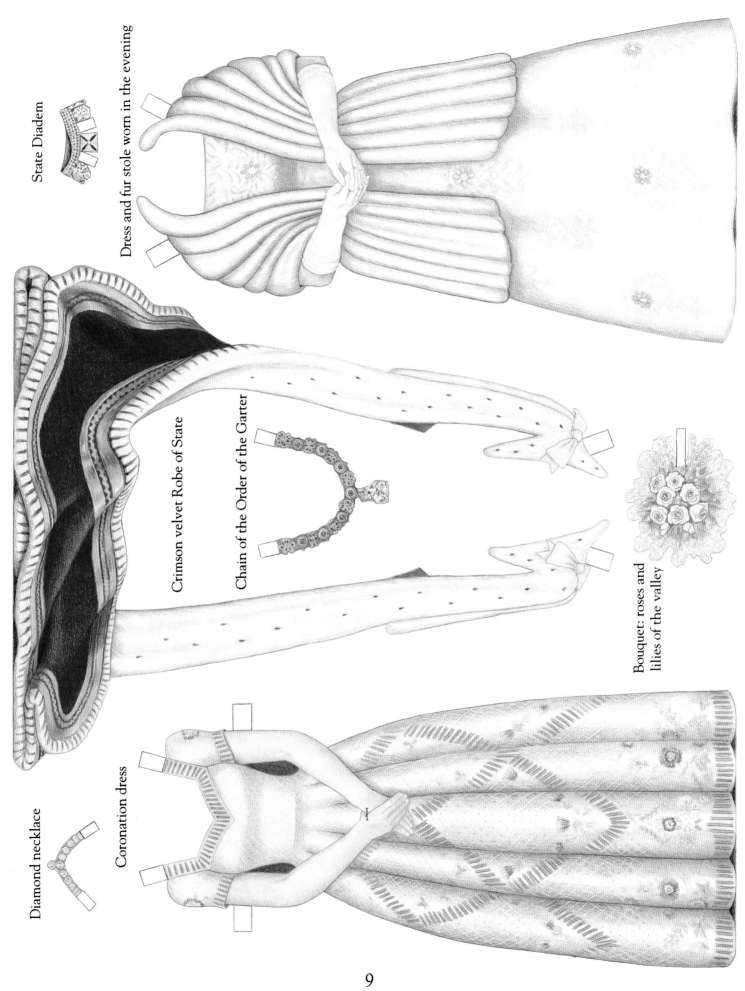

State Diadem

Dress and fur stole worn in the evening

Crimson velvet Robe of State

Chain of the Order of the Garter

Bouquet: roses and lilies of the valley

Diamond necklace

Coronation dress

Earl Marshal
wearing peer's robe

Supertunica worn over Colobium Sindonis

White overdress worn for
the Anointing

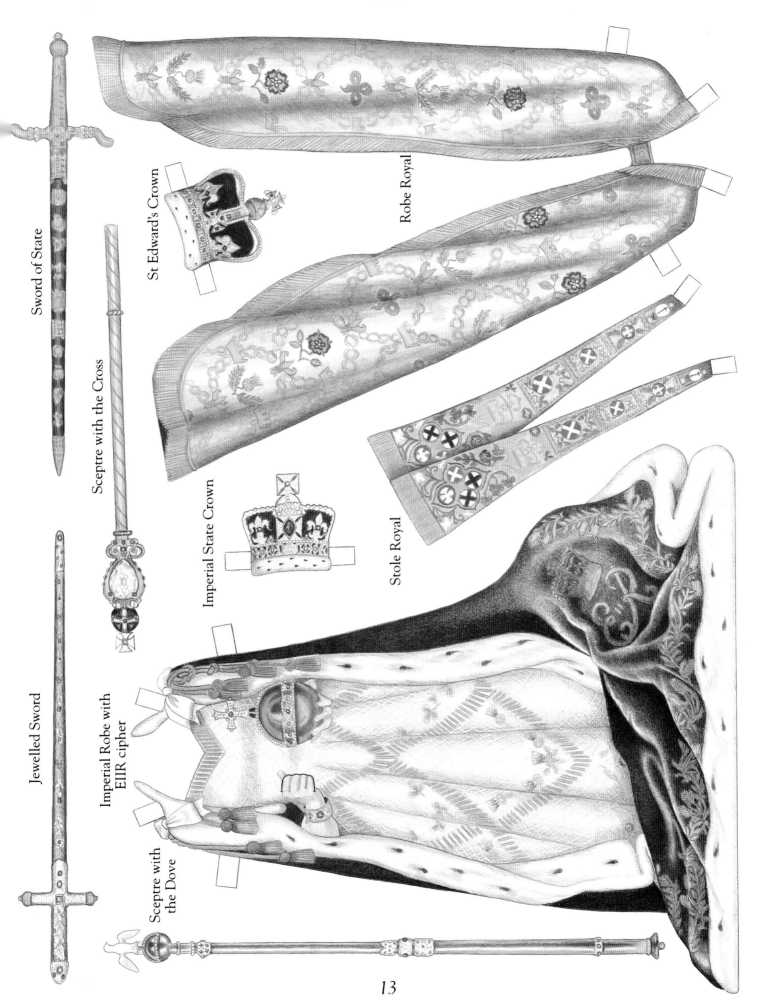

Sword of State

St Edward's Crown

Robe Royal

Sceptre with the Cross

Imperial State Crown

Stole Royal

Jewelled Sword

Imperial Robe with
EIIR cipher

Sceptre with
the Dove

EIIR

cut

cut

Her Majesty
Queen Elizabeth II

fold here

fold here

cut

cut

15

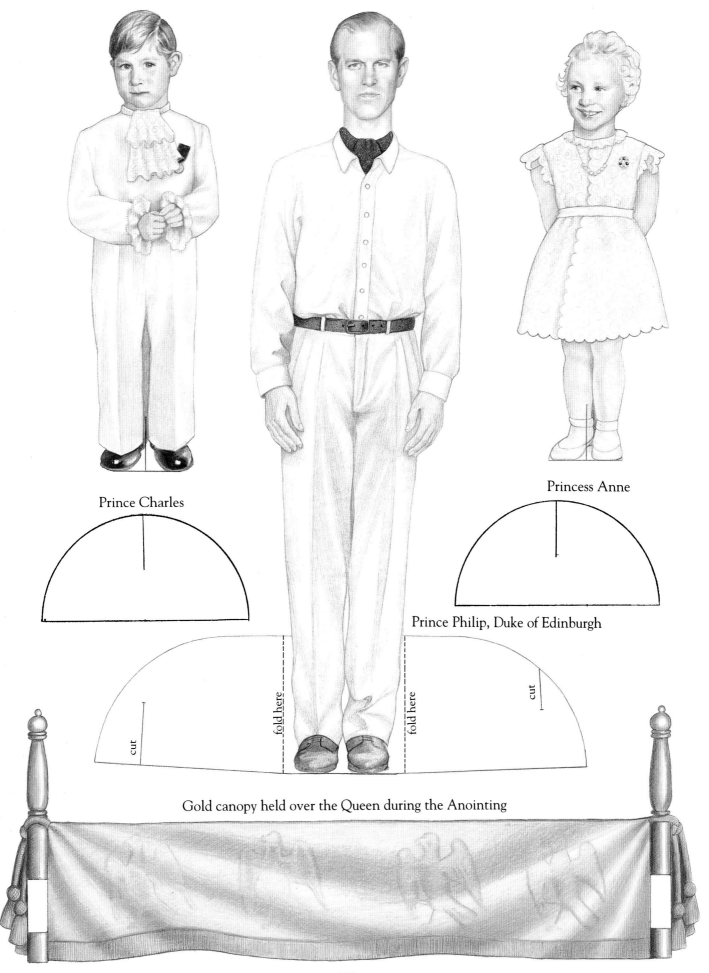

Prince Charles

Princess Anne

Prince Philip, Duke of Edinburgh

fold here

fold here

cut

cut

Gold canopy held over the Queen during the Anointing

—

Duke of Edinburgh's evening dress, 1953

Peer's robe with chain and badge of the Order of the Garter, worn by the Duke at the Coronation

Duke's coronet

Admiral's bicorne hat

Admiral's sword

Full dress uniform, Admiral of the Fleet

Maid of Honour

Queen Elizabeth the Queen Mother

Princess Margaret

cut

cut

cut

Windsor Herald

cut

cut

cut

Archbishop of Canterbury

Dean of Westminster with cushion for St Edward's Crown

THE CROWN JEWELS

THE BRITISH MONARCHY possesses some of the finest jewellery in the world. The Queen herself, like her grandmother Queen Mary, is a knowledgeable and discriminating collector. However, the jewels and rich treasures used in the coronation ceremony are not just precious, beautiful objects. They all have a special meaning as well.

The word "coronation" comes from the Latin word for "crown". The moment when the Archbishop of Canterbury placed the crown on Queen Elizabeth's head was the high point of the coronation ceremony. The Archbishop used St Edward's Crown. It is over 300 years old and was made for the coronation of King Charles II in 1661. It contains gold from earlier royal crowns, as well as many magnificent stones. Later on in the ceremony, the Queen wore the lighter Imperial State Crown, made for Queen Victoria's coronation in 1838 and used for coronations ever since. The Imperial State Crown contains the "Black Prince's Ruby" (actually a different precious stone called a spinel) that is reputed to have been worn by Henry V at the Battle of Agincourt and which may have belonged before that to the Black Prince. The crown also contains a sapphire from the original St Edward's Crown, which had been destroyed during the Civil War; the Second Star of Africa diamond, one of the four stars cut from the Cullinan diamond (the largest diamond ever found); and pearls that belonged to Queen Elizabeth I. In addition there were four rubies, seventeen sapphires, eleven emeralds, 277 pearls and no fewer than 3,000 smaller diamonds.

Other royal treasures known as the "Regalia" were presented to the Queen at various times during the coronation ceremony as symbols of her powers and responsibilities as Sovereign. (You can see some of them on page 13.) These included the Golden Spurs (which represent honour and chivalry); the Jewelled Sword (honour); the Sword of State (majesty and authority); the Armills (bracelets of wisdom and sincerity); the Orb with the Cross (God's power over the world); the Ring of Kingly Dignity (represents the wedding of the Sovereign with her people); the Sceptre with the Cross (power and justice); and the Sceptre with the Dove (fairness and mercy). Before the ceremony, the Regalia was guarded by twenty-one Beefeaters and fifty Grenadier Guards. Afterwards, they were returned for safe keeping to their "home" in the Tower of London.

The Queen's Clothes

O N CORONATION DAY, the Queen wore a great many different clothes and jewels. They were all sumptuous and beautiful, and they were all designed to make a public statement about her royal dignity and rank. The Queen arrived at Westminster Abbey wearing the George IV State Diadem and the Robe of State. The State Diadem is familiar to millions of people, since the Queen is shown wearing it on British postage stamps. The diadem is shaped like a crown and sparkles with diamonds. The Robe of State was made for Queen Victoria and was worn not only by her at her coronation in 1838, but also by Queen Elizabeth the Queen Mother at the coronation of George VI in 1937. It is made of white and black ermine fur and crimson silk velvet. The train is six metres long and over one metre wide. Once the coronation service began, the Queen removed this historic robe and the State Diadem. They were not worn again during the ceremony.

Other clothes were made especially for the occasion. Norman Hartnell, the leading British designer who had made the then Princess Elizabeth's wedding dress in 1947, was asked to make the coronation dress and all the other dresses worn by royal ladies at the ceremony. It was a great honour and a great responsibility. He suggested eight different designs for the coronation dress alone. The Queen and Prince Philip discussed, and suggested improvements to, the design that was finally chosen.

The dress was made of white silk satin with a low neck, short sleeves, a tightly fitted waist and a long skirt. The silk of the dress was embroidered all over in coloured silks and gold and silver metal thread, crystal, pearls and opals in a design incorporating eleven floral emblems. The flowers represented the countries of which the Queen is sovereign. The skirt of the dress was stiffened by a tafetta lining reinforced with horsehair so that depsite the weight of the embroidery, the dress would hang straight and move gracefully. The final effect was rich and colourful and certainly majestic. Wearing it, the Queen resembled one of the portraits of her namesake, Queen Elizabeth I, who reigned during the 16th century and was famous for her splendid jewelled clothes.

The 1953 coronation dress took has never been valued, but must be worth hundreds of thousands of pounds. Today, it is kept in the Tower of London along with the other Crown Jewels. Some of the Queen's coronation clothes had a religious purpose, like the simple white overdress that she wore for the ceremony of Anointing (sprinkling with holy oil). This demonstrated her humility before God. It was also a useful garment, since it covered the exquisite coronation dress and prevented the oil from dripping on the satin and jewels. Throughout the ceremony, the Queen was helped into and out of her different clothes by her six Maids of Honour, who were young, unmarried women from among the oldest, most aristocratic families in the land. The Dowager Duchess of Devonshire was Mistress of the Robes. She was responsible for their safe keeping, and for making sure they were ready for the Queen to wear at the right moment in the ceremony. She was assisted by several young pages, and by the Groom of the Robes.

Certain royal clothes have been worn at coronations for many centuries. After the Anointing, the Queen's white overdress was removed and the Queen was clothed in these traditional garments: firstly, the Colobium Sindonis (a sleeveless white linen tunic), the Supertunica (like a long coat with wide sleeves made of cloth-of-gold, tied at the waist by a golden girdle); the Stole Royal (a long, embroidered scarf), and the wonderful, glittering Robe Royal. This mantle of cloth-of-gold made the Queen look, as one observer wrote, "like a statue of precious metal".

The Queen was crowned wearing all this finery, but, before she left the Abbey, the traditional garments were removed. Her Maids of Honour helped her put on her own new purple Imperial Robe, made, like the Robe of State that the Queen had worn before being crowned, of velvet and ermine. It was trimmed with heavy gold tassels, and embroidered with a design of golden olive branches and ears of corn. These stood for "peace" and "plenty". The robe also bore the Queen's cipher, "E II R". This shortened form of her royal title – it stands for "Elizabetha II Regina", which is Latin for Queen Elizabeth II – is used on all kinds of government documents, from royal proclamations to income tax forms. Wearing the Imperial State Crown, the Queen walked in solemn procession out of the Abbey, and, smiling radiantly, stepped into her coach for the ride home.

When the Queen appeared on the balcony of Buckingham Palace to wave to the crowd of 150,000 packed into the wide street outside its gates, she was dressed, at first, exactly as she had been when she left the Abbey. Then she reappeared without the purple Imperial Robe. It was too awkward and heavy to wear for very long. Later that evening, she appeared once more, this time to switch on the power for a dramatic floodlit display. She wore a jewelled evening dress, the State Diadem, and, because it was a cold evening, a warm fur stole.

The coronation ceremony was televised, so the Queen needed to pay special attention to her make-up. The colours had to be bright enough to stop her looking pale under the artificial lights. Expert make-up artists were called in. They advised the Queen to wear deep shades to add impact to her naturally delicate colouring; she has a fair skin, mid-brown hair and dark blue eyes. These were the colours they chose: a peach foundation, red-blue rouge, light brown mascara and red lipstick with a definite blue undertone. This was far more make-up than the Queen usually wore. "Remember that I am not a film star," she said.

PRINCE AND PEERS

BEFORE HE MARRIED THE QUEEN, Prince Philip had been an officer in the Royal Navy. During the Second World War, he served with the Mediterranean Fleet on a naval gunboat, and he had planned to make his peacetime career with ships and the sea. After his marriage, this was no longer possible. He had a new, difficult and delicate career as Consort of the Queen.

During the war, Prince Philip had won promotion steadily on his own merits. Now, as a member of the royal family, he was given a special senior rank, Admiral of the Fleet. It was decided that he should attend the coronation wearing the magnificent full-dress Admiral's uniform. It was based on an early 19th-century design. The trousers are long, straight and close fitting, and are worn with a short, high-necked jacket, tailored in navy blue and trimmed with gold buttons and braid. Its shoulders were ornamented with magnificent epaulettes made of heavy gold cord. Pinned to his uniform were rows of medals the Prince had won on active service. He also wore the ribbon, chain and badge of the Order of the Garter, a select group of nights and nobles dating back to medieval times. He carried an admiral's bicorne hat and a splendid ceremonial sword.

When he married, Prince Philip was created Duke of Edinburgh, a title last given to Queen Victoria's second son. Like all the other peers – dukes, marquises, earls and barons – the Duke was summoned to attend the coronation wearing a peer's robe. Even the Duke of Norfolk, as Earl Marshal, was required to wear his peer's robe and coronet over his court costume of satin shirt, knee-breeches and long white stockings. Peers' robes are made of crimson velvet, trimmed with fur. The amount of fur varies according to rank; dukes have the most, barons the least. Properly, ermine should be used, but it is very expensive. Since peers had to pay for their own robes, many made do with rabbit fur, bleached and dyed to look like ermine. A typical robe cost £245, about six months' wages at that time for an ordinary worker.

ROYAL LADIES

FOR THE CORONATION, as always, the Queen Mother took great care with her appearance. Her dress, designed by Norman Hartnell, was rich and splendid, but, thoughtfully, did not outshine her daughter's clothes. Like the new Queen, the Queen Mother chose white silk for her dress, which was embroidered with gold metal thread and diamantés and had a broad band of gold silk at the hem. The design for the embroidery was based on elegant fronds of ostrich feathers, used for many centuries as a symbol of royalty and power. Over this, the Queen Mother wore a velvet robe lined with fur. It had a long train, which needed four page boys to carry. She also wore a broad blue sash to show that she was a member of the Order of the Garter. On her head, she had a diadem glittering with diamonds. She wore a magnificent diamond necklace and many beautiful brooches.

Princess Margaret was only twenty two when her older sister was crowned. The young princess was widely admired for her dramatic good looks. (It was also rumoured that she was in love with a dashing former airman, Peter Townsend.) She wore a dress of white silk satin embroidered from waist to hem with pearls, crystals and silver metal thread in a design of roses and daisies. This was a gentle joke – the French word for "daisy" is "marguerite", and "margarita" is also another name for "pearl". The finished effect was lovely. As Norman Hartnell himself described it, "she moved in white beauty...." Princess Margaret arrived at the Abbey wearing a glittering diamond tiara. Later in the ceremony, she wore a coronet lined with fur-trimmed purple velvet.

The six Maids of Honour also wore white dresses designed by Hartnell. They were made of satin, patterned with golden sequins. Unlike the other coronation clothes, these dresses were not lined. One of the Maids of Honour described them as beautiful, but rather prickly to wear. The Maids of Honour had wreaths of white artificial flowers in their carefully-arranged hair, pearl necklaces, and – like all women except the Queen – long white gloves.

CHURCH AND STATE

THE QUEEN'S CORONATION took place in church and was, at least in part, a deeply religious ceremony. Several clergymen officiated, led by the Archbishop of Canterbury, the most senior churchman in England. For the first time ever, the leading Scottish clergyman, the Moderator of the General Assembly of the Church of Scotland, was also invited to take part. At an early stage in the ceremony, he presented a copy of the Bible to the Queen.

Like the coronation service itself, the robes worn by most of these clergymen followed an ancient, traditional pattern. The bishops and archbishop were dressed in long, straight, black robes called cassocks, covered with flowing white surplices. Over these, they wore long, embroidered stoles – like silk scarves with fringed ends – and magnificent floor-length copes. A cope is a cloak made of silk and often richly embroidered with coloured silks and silver and gold metal thread in beautiful designs that have religious significance. For example, the Archbishop of Canterbury's cope has a pattern of vine leaves, which are symbols of Jesus's life and death.

The Heralds, who helped the Earl Marshal arrange and oversee the coronation ceremony, were also dressed in traditional clothes. They wore brilliant heraldic tabards, tunics patterned with the Royal Arms. These elaborate pictures, called "devices", developed from the patterns used by medieval knights to decorate their shields so they could be easily identified when wearing armour. The Royal Arms symbolize Great Britain. They show the leopards of England, the Scottish lion and the Irish harp.

The Welsh dragon device is used by the Prince of Wales, a title reserved for the monarch's eldest son. Prince Charles, aged four, attended his mother's coronation dressed in a suit of white satin trimmed with lace. His younger sister, Princess Anne, was reported to be very unhappy when she was left behind. But she was allowed to appear on the balcony at Buckingham Palace after the ceremony.

THE SERVICE

EVERY ENGLISH MONARCH since William the Conqueror (1066–1087) has been crowned, except Edward V, who was murdered, and Edward VIII, who gave up his right to be king. Elizabeth II was the thirty ninth monarch to be crowned at Westminster, and the thirty first to be crowned in Westminster Abbey. The Abbey was begun in the reign of Henry II (1216–1242). It stands on the site of an earlier church founded by King Edward the Confessor. He reigned from 1042–1066, and is the only English king to have been made a saint. The Abbey's senior clergyman, the Dean, plays an important part in each coronation service, assisting the Archbishop of Canterbury, who crowns the Queen, and the Bishops of Durham and Bath and Wells, who traditionally support the Queen throughout the ceremony.

The coronation service, like the site of the coronation, has remained much the same for over 1,000 years. In 1953, Queen Elizabeth's coronation carefully followed ancient tradition. First came the Recognition. The Queen was presented to the people four times, to which they replied, "God Save Queen Elizabeth". Then the Queen took the Oath, a solemn promise to govern according to the law and to protect the church. In preparation for the anointing ceremony, the Queen took her seat in King Edward's Chair, made in 1300 for her ancestor, Edward I. She was anointed with holy oil to show that she was dedicated to God. After this, she was invested with the Regalia, each item designed to remind her of her important duties as Queen.

At last came the moment of Coronation. The Archbishop of Canterbury lifted the crown high in the air, then gently placed it on the Queen's head. Everyone shouted "God Save the Queen". Trumpets and drums sounded in triumph, mingling the roar of gunfire from the Tower of London and Hyde Park. Then she received the Homage. All the nobles of England, beginning with her husband, Prince Philip, knelt before her, promising to live and die in her service. Finally, the newly crowned Queen received Holy Communion. Her coronation had been magnificently achieved.